STAR BIOGRAPHIES

CHRIS PRATT

KENNY ABDO

Fly!
An Imprint of Abdo Zoom
abdobooks.com

abdobooks.com

Published by Abdo Zoom, a division of ABDO, P.O. Box 398166, Minneapolis, Minnesota 55439. Copyright © 2019 by Abdo Consulting Group, Inc. International copyrights reserved in all countries. No part of this book may be reproduced in any form without written permission from the publisher. Fly!™ is a trademark and logo of Abdo Zoom.

Printed in the United States of America, North Mankato, Minnesota.
092018
012019

THIS BOOK CONTAINS
RECYCLED MATERIALS

Photo Credits: Alamy, AP Images, Everette Collection, Getty Images, iStock, newscom, Seth Poppel/Yearbook Library, Shutterstock
Production Contributors: Kenny Abdo, Jennie Forsberg, Grace Hansen
Design Contributors: Dorothy Toth, Neil Klinepier

Library of Congress Control Number: 2018946252

Publisher's Cataloging–in–Publication Data

Names: Abdo, Kenny, author.
Title: Chris Pratt / by Kenny Abdo.
Description: Minneapolis, Minnesota : Abdo Zoom, 2019 | Series: Star biographies
    | Includes online resources and index.
Identifiers: ISBN 9781532125430 (lib. bdg.) | ISBN 9781641856881 (pbk) |
    ISBN 9781532126451 (ebook) | ISBN 9781532126963 (Read-to-me ebook)
Subjects: LCSH: Pratt, Chris, 1979- --Juvenile literature. | Actors--United States--
    Biography--Juvenile literature. | Motion picture actors and actresses--
    Biography--Juvenile literature.
Classification: DDC 792.028092 [B]--dc23

TABLE OF CONTENTS

CHRIS PRATT

Blowing up on the big and small screen, Chris Pratt has made the leap into mega-stardom! Pratt makes the world laugh in popular TV comedies and **blockbuster** movies.

EARLY YEARS

Christopher Michael Pratt was born in Virginia, Minnesota, in 1979.

Canada

VIRGINIA ■

North Dakota

Minnesota

Wisconsin

South Dakota

Iowa

His family moved to Lake Stevens, Washington, when he was three years old. He enjoyed wrestling in high school.

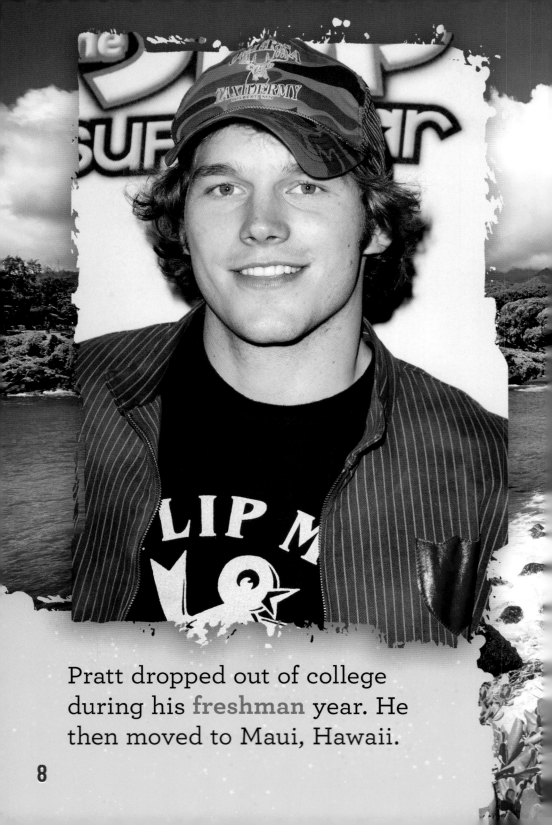

Pratt dropped out of college during his **freshman** year. He then moved to Maui, Hawaii.

THE BIG TIME

Pratt spent the next few years homeless, living out of a van. While working as a waiter, he was discovered by a director and got his first acting **gig**.

Pratt got his big break on the TV show *Everwood* in 2002. He auditioned for what was supposed to be a guest spot on *Parks and Recreation* in 2009. His character, Andy, was so popular, he became a cast regular.

His first major movie **role** was in *Moneyball* in 2011. He trained to play professional baseball for the part. Usually right-handed, he learned to bat left-handed.

After many supporting roles, he became a leading man with his voice in 2014's *The Lego Movie*. That same year he played Star-Lord in Marvel's hit *Guardians of the Galaxy*.

Jurassic World came out in 2015. It ended up earning more than $1 billion dollars at the **box office**. Pratt became a worldwide star.

LEGACY

Pratt was named one of the 100 most **influential** people in the world by *TIME Magazine* in 2015.

Pratt volunteers his time visiting **terminally ill** children. Sometimes he will surprise the kids at charity screenings of his films and watch the movies with them.

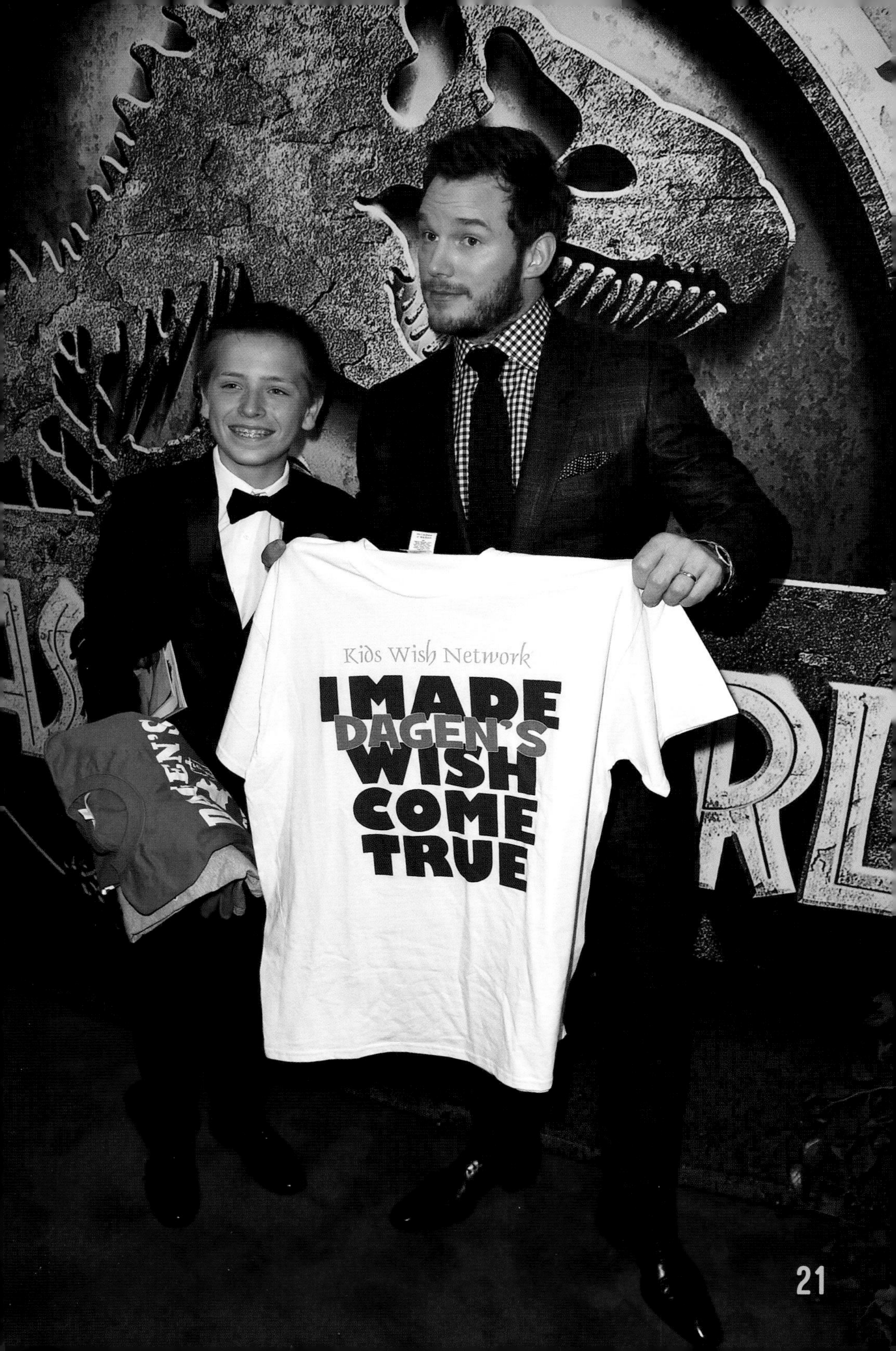
Kids Wish Network
I MADE
DAGEN'S
WISH
COME
TRUE

GLOSSARY

audition – a trial performance showcasing personal talent as a musician, singer, dancer, or actor.

blockbuster – a movie that is a big commercial success.

box office – referring to the commercial success of a movie in terms of audience size.

freshman – a first-year student.

gig – a job, usually referring to entertainment.

influential – someone who has a strong influence over people or things.

role – a part an actor plays.

terminally ill – being incurably sick.

ONLINE RESOURCES

Booklinks
NONFICTION NETWORK
FREE! ONLINE NONFICTION RESOURCES

To learn more about Chris Pratt, please visit abdobooklinks.com. These links are routinely monitored and updated to provide the most current information available.

INDEX